# Defying Death and Time: Mummies

by K. Simpson

**Scott Foresman**
is an imprint of

**PEARSON**

Glenview, Illinois • Boston, Massachusetts • Chandler, Arizona •
Upper Saddle River, New Jersey

**Illustrations**
**8** Albert Lorenz.

**Photographs**
Every effort has been made to secure permission and provide appropriate credit for photographic material. The publisher deeply regrets any omission and pledges to correct errors called to its attention in subsequent editions.

Unless otherwise acknowledged, all photographs are the property of Pearson Education, Inc.

Photo locators denoted as follows: Top (T), Center (C), Bottom (B), Left (L), Right (R), Background (Bkgd)

**Opener** Brian Lawrence/PhotoLibrary Group, Inc.; **1** Cris Bouroncle/APF/Getty Images; **5** Supreme Council of Antiquities/©AP Images; **6** Sandro Vannini/Corbis; **7** Roger Wood/Corbis; **9** (TR) Brian Lawrence/PhotoLibrary Group, Inc., (CR) Michael Nicholson/Corbis; **10** Ben Curtis/Getty Images; **11** Sandro Vannini/Corbis; **13** Supreme Council Of Antiquities/Corbis; **14** Gary Cook/Alamy Images; **15** Cris Bouroncle/APF/Getty Images; **17** (BL) Discovery Channel/HO/©AP Images, (R) JD. Dallet/PhotoLibrary Group, Inc.; **18** Nasser Nuri/Reuters Media; **19** ©Ivy Close Images/Alamy; **20** (Inset) Reza/Webistan/Corbis, (TL) Tim Simond/Alamy Images; **22** Sandro Vannini/Corbis.

ISBN 13: 978-0-328-52561-4
ISBN 10:     0-328-52561-8

**Copyright © by Pearson Education, Inc., or its affiliates.** All rights reserved. Printed in the United States of America. This publication is protected by copyright, and permission should be obtained from the publisher prior to any prohibited reproduction, storage in a retrieval system, or transmission in any form or by any means, electronic, mechanical, photocopying, recording, or likewise. For information regarding permissions, write to Pearson Curriculum Rights & Permissions, One Lake Street, Upper Saddle River, New Jersey 07458.

**Pearson®** is a trademark, in the U.S. and/or in other countries, of Pearson plc or its affiliates.
**Scott Foresman®** is a trademark, in the U.S. and/or in other countries, of Pearson Education, Inc., or its affiliates.

2 3 4 5 6 7 8 9 10 V0N4 13 12 11 10

# Table of Contents

**Chapter 1 .................................................................... 4**
**The Science of the Past**

**Chapter 2 .................................................................... 7**
**The Valley of the Kings and the Search for Tutankhamen**

**Chapter 3 .................................................................. 11**
**A Lucky Find**

**Chapter 4 .................................................................. 15**
**A Mummy Gone Missing**

**Chapter 5 .................................................................. 19**
**Not Every Mummy Comes from Egypt**

Now Try This ................................................................ 22

# Chapter 1 The Science of the Past

A man descends into an underground chamber cut out of a white limestone hillside. Behind him, a wooden staircase climbs up to ground level, supported along the way by stacks of sandbags. The man makes his way down another shaft, farther into the hillside. He peers excitedly through a hole chopped out of a limestone wall. Before him is a room full of what looks like rubble: broken stone jars, a dirty painted mask, strands of brown cloth, and five ancient, splintering coffins.

The man can hardly contain his excitement. He isn't a grave robber looking for age-old treasures. This man is an archaeologist, a scientist who studies **artifacts** of the distant past. He is in Egypt's Valley of the Kings to learn more about the people of ancient Egypt. He is especially interested in those who hoped to defy both death and time by having their bodies mummified for the afterlife.

Death, some say, is the ultimate equalizer. It doesn't matter who you are, whether you are rich or poor, powerful or humble, Eastern or Western. All living beings eventually die. In ancient Egypt, however, death was not much of an equalizer.

Ancient Egyptians believed in a life after death in which they would return to their bodies. The wealthiest and most powerful members of Egyptian society were buried with everything they might need or want in the afterlife. Some spent decades building their tombs, decorating them with paintings and carvings, and filling them with food, drink, furniture, jewelry, and even animals. When death finally arrived, experts whisked their bodies away for mummification.

It was not a simple process. First, the body had to be **embalmed**—treated to prevent decay. Experts washed the body with special products and performed religious

**Archaeologists uncover a tomb discovered in the Valley of the Kings, near Luxor, Egypt.**

ceremonies to purify it. They surgically removed most internal organs, including the liver, intestines, stomach, lungs, and brain. These organs were placed in special containers, called canopic jars. The jars were considered sacred and were placed inside the tomb with the mummy.

5

Next, experts covered the body with a salt called natron in a special drying process to preserve tissue. After a couple of months had passed, the skin shriveled and darkened, and the body no longer resembled a living person. To make it look more lifelike, embalmers plumped it up with sawdust and other materials. After all, a **pharaoh** needed to look good for his (or her) entrance into the afterlife! Embalmers then cleaned the body and rubbed it with oils and perfumes. Finally, they wrapped it in linen, tucking jewels and charms between the layers. After great fanfare and a religious ceremony, the mummy was taken to its tomb and sealed inside.

This is a process that ancient Egyptians used for mummification, and Chapters 2 through 4 will focus on examples of royal Egyptian mummies. But not all mummies were pharaohs, nor were they all Egyptians. Mummies have been discovered in many parts of the world. Some were wealthy and powerful; some were not. In some cases, weather and time mummified bodies accidentally! Chapter 5 will deal with these "accidental" mummies.

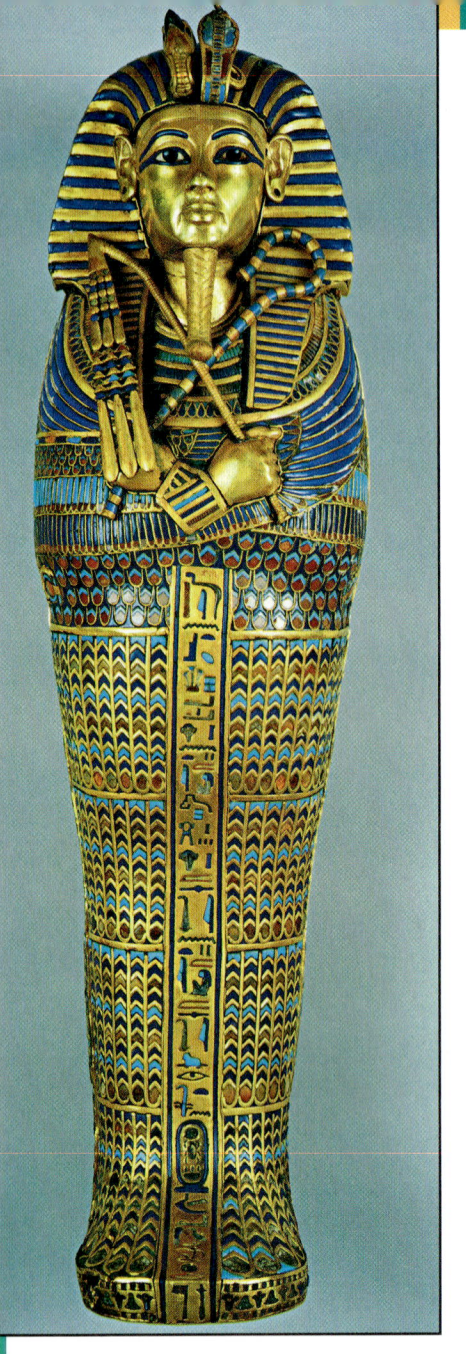

The mummy of Pharaoh Tutankhamen was placed inside three nested coffins before burial. In this photo you see his outer coffin, also called a *sarcophagus*.

Egypt's Valley of the Kings

## Chapter 2  The Valley of the Kings and the Search for Tutankhamen

The Nile River has long been an **artery** of trade through Egypt, busily transporting people and goods. A few miles from this crowded river, ancient pharaohs chose a long, crooked valley for their entrance into the afterlife. For about five hundred years, this valley was where Egyptians buried their pharaohs. Many archaeologists speculate that pharaohs chose this place because they believed thieves might not find it.

This is a valley of secrets; tombs here do not lie beneath impressive pyramids. These pharaohs carved their final resting places out of the rocky hills. Some tombs were fairly humble; some were never finished; some were magnificent. This place is now known as the Valley of the Kings. So far, more than sixty tombs have been **excavated**, but almost all of them had been looted in ancient times. The one exception so far is the tomb of Tutankhamen.

Tutankhamen was a boy king who began his reign in 1333 BCE when he was nine or ten years old. Adults helped him rule for the next ten years or so, until his death around the age of eighteen. When Tutankhamen died, he was mummified to help him succeed in his life after death.

Soon after his burial, robbers opened Tutankhamen's tomb, but officials caught them red-handed, put the royal treasures back, and quickly resealed the tomb. After that, the boy king's mummy lay peacefully lost in the Valley of the Kings for thirty-three centuries. Even with tomb robbers, archaeologists, and treasure seekers looking for it, Tutankhamen's tomb remained undisturbed until 1922.

An Englishman named Howard Carter spent years hunting for Tutankhamen's tomb. He had nearly reached the last of his funding when a boy spotted the top of a buried staircase while carrying water to Carter's workers. He showed it to Carter, proving that scientific discovery is sometimes as much about luck as it is about expertise.

Carter ordered the men to uncover the staircase. Digging carefully, they found a corridor at its foot and then a sealed entrance to a tomb. In the late afternoon of November 26, 1922, Carter made a hole in the stone doorway and peered into the chamber.

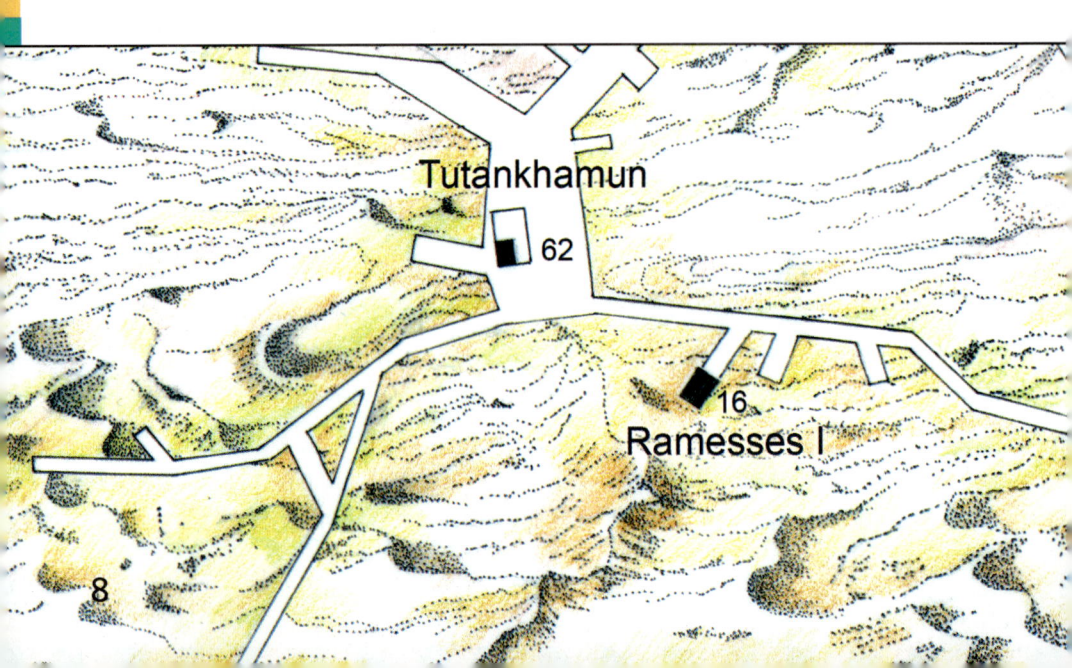

Carter later wrote:

*At first I could see nothing, the hot air escaping from the chamber causing the candle flame to flicker, but presently, as my eyes grew accustomed to the light, details of the room within emerged slowly from the mist, strange animals, statues and gold—everywhere the glint of gold.*

What Carter found inside was stunning—a corridor and four chambers with fantastically painted walls. Gold and precious stones covered thousands of objects, including chariots, furniture, lamps, and jewelry. Most spectacular of all was Tutankhamen himself, mummified, inside three nested coffins. A gold mask decorated with glass and semiprecious stones covered the boy king's face.

Artifacts in Tutankhamen's tomb told archaeologists a good deal about the splendid lifestyles of Egyptian royals.

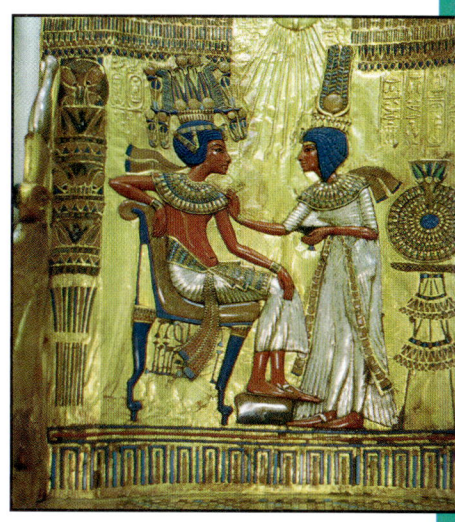

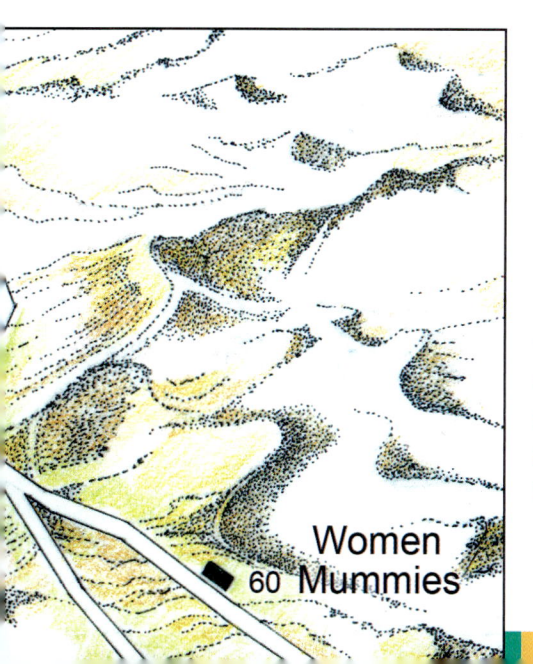

This is a map of a section of the Valley of the Kings where the tombs of Tutankhamun, Rameses I, and two unidentified women were found.

Women 60 Mummies

9

Archaeologists in the 1920s routinely unwrapped mummies, sometimes cutting them apart to get a better look. The embalming fluids that had protected Tutankhamen from decay for so many centuries also caused the gold mask to stick to his face. To remove it, Carter's men decapitated the mummy and pried off the mask with hot knives. Today's archaeologists use methods that are not as **intrusive**, including sophisticated scanning equipment and DNA science.

Occasionally, Egyptian officials have authorized a viewing of the young pharaoh, allowing the world to see him and—if you share the ancient Egyptians' belief in an afterlife—allowing him to see the world.

**Archaeologists study the mummy of Tutankhamen.**

Walls inside the tomb of Ramesses I were painted with extravagant murals.

## Chapter 3  A Lucky Find

Three thousand years ago, Ramesses I ruled Egypt for about two years. Although his reign was short, he was an important leader because his children and grandchildren rose to be among the most **influential** pharaohs in Egypt's history.

Upon his death, Ramesses I was mummified and sealed in his royal tomb. Over the next several centuries, tomb robbing was a big problem in the Valley of the Kings. Finally, about four hundred years after Ramesses' burial, caretakers moved his mummy, along with dozens of others, into one tomb, hidden in rugged hillsides near the city of Deir el-Bahri. There it rested for more than twenty-seven centuries, until an Egyptian man named Ahmed lost a goat in the mid-1800s.

Once again, an archaeological discovery depended on luck. While looking for his goat, Ahmed Abd el-Rassul scrambled around the cliffs. There he found the tomb holding Ramesses I. In fact, Ahmed found not only Ramesses, but also all the treasures and mummies that had been hidden in that secret tomb for 2,700 years.

What happened next is a bit fuzzy. Ahmed and his family gained a reputation for selling artifacts, including mummies, from royal tombs. So it is no surprise that they were eventually caught by authorities. Most family members refused to talk about where the artifacts came from, but one person finally did, and the secret tomb was officially "discovered" in 1881. Ramesses' coffin was there, **inscribed** with his name, but it was empty.

Did Ahmed's family sell the mummy? No one knows for sure, but we know that a Canadian doctor who traveled to Egypt at around the same time purchased several mummies from an unknown source. The doctor bought the mummies for a man he knew who owned a museum (of sorts) in Niagara Falls. The museum wasn't the kind of place that would have an Egyptologist, an expert on Egypt's history, on its staff. In fact, it specialized in tacky tourist attractions, such as the barrels that daredevils had used to ride over Niagara Falls.

For the next 140 years, the mummies stayed in that museum, where they frightened children and were gawked at by tourists. Egyptologists heard about them, and some even came to have a look. In the 1980s, a few experts who had seen the mummies wondered if one of them in particular might be a pharaoh. Its powerful size and resemblance to other royal mummies was striking. The notion that a pharaoh's mummy might be resting in a glass case at Niagara Falls seemed ridiculous, but intriguing.

In 1999 the Niagara Falls museum closed, and its owners sold the mummy to a museum

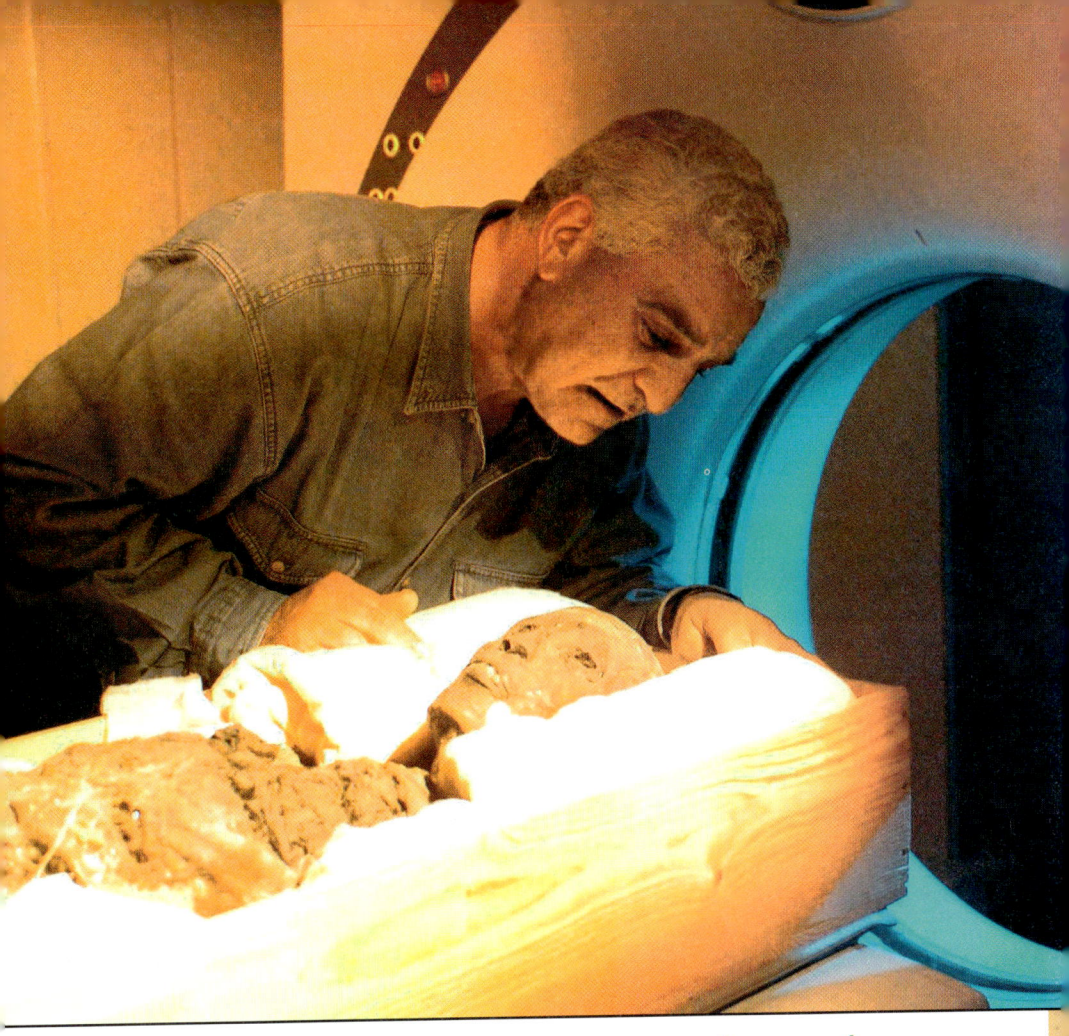

Modern archaeologists use CT scanners to examine mummies.

in Atlanta, Georgia. Egyptologists in Atlanta knew that the mummy was special. They studied it with great care, using X-ray and CT scanning technology. A CT scan offers a **cross-sectioned** view, allowing scientists to see tissue and bone both inside and outside the body.

The Egyptologists found that the mummy's arms were folded across the chest in the position used by Egyptian royalty. From the condition of the skin, they knew that the mummification process had been of high quality, as it would have been for a pharaoh. Experts also realized that the mummy looked like several other mummies, all members of Ramesses' family.

Suspicions grew that this mummy was Ramesses I, and this presented a problem. Ramesses' mummy had been stolen from his tomb. If this was Ramesses, Egypt had a rightful claim of ownership, and ownership was a sensitive issue for many Egyptians.

Archaeologists, explorers, and even hobbyists had long considered it their right to take artifacts from Egypt whenever they wanted. Laws in their own countries supported them—the doctor who brought Ramesses I to Canada broke no Canadian laws. Because he had paid for the mummy, he owned it. Yet Egyptians considered these artifacts part of their culture and regarded them as the property of Egypt. Egyptian officials requested that museums around the world return Egypt's artifacts. Worldwide, attitudes about who rightfully owns historical artifacts were changing. The museum in Atlanta was caught in the middle.

Although the mummy had not been clearly identified as Ramesses I, the Michael C. Carlos Museum in Atlanta decided to return it to the Luxor Museum in Egypt. In 2003 the mummy finally went home. A children's choir sang songs of welcome.

**A mummy on display in Luxor Museum**

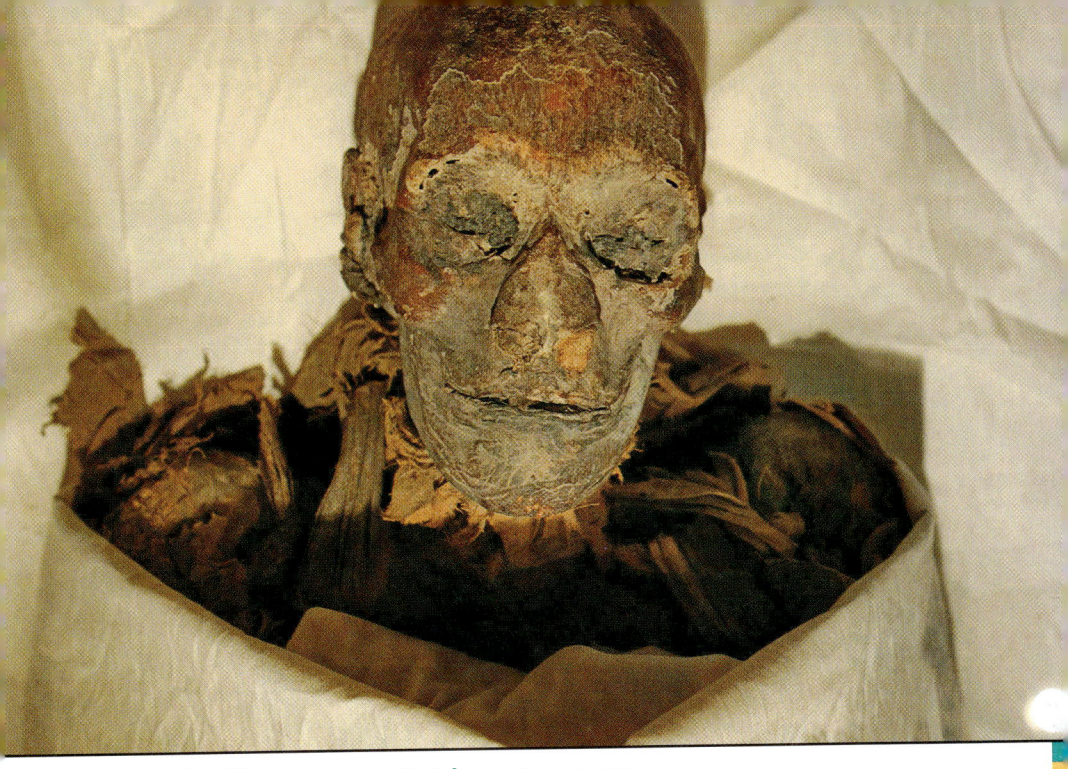

Around 3,500 years ago, Hatshepsut was one of Egypt's most powerful pharaohs.

## Chapter 4  A Mummy Gone Missing

Before Ramesses I and before Tutankhamen, there was Hatshepsut. She was thought to be the most powerful woman in Egypt's long history of powerful women. After her father's death in 1492 BCE, Hatshepsut ruled Egypt alongside her half brother until he too died. After that, she co-ruled with her young stepson Thutmose III, though Thutmose III had little real power. Hatshepsut eventually stole the throne from her stepson, declaring herself pharaoh.

Hatshepsut's place in Egyptian history is unique. There had been a few female pharaohs before her, but only when a male heir to the throne was not available. In her world, rulers were usually men. This may have been why she dressed as a man and wore the false beard that male pharaohs traditionally wore. She also called herself by titles that were usually reserved for men.

For twenty-two years, she ruled Egypt with a confident and powerful hand, sending grand expeditions to faraway lands and bringing great wealth home to Egypt. Putting this wealth to work, she commissioned extravagant buildings, including a temple in her name at Deir el Bahri, which is still known as one of the finest examples of ancient Egyptian architecture.

Hatshepsut became one of the great pharaohs, broadening Egypt's territory, expanding trade with other countries, ordering beautiful artwork, and settling arguments between religious and political leaders. Some scholars suggest that the famous female pharaoh Cleopatra would look to Hatshepsut as a role model, several centuries later.

In the end, though, Thutmose III may have had revenge on his stepmother. The death of Hatshepsut remains mysterious. After her death, statues of her were smashed. Her name was erased from Egyptian writings, and her image removed from buildings. Her mummy was nowhere to be found. It was only in the 1800s that archaeologists finally began to understand her role in history. They learned about her by piecing together clues and smashed artifacts.

As the years rolled by, every Egyptologist knew that two female mummies lay on the floor of the tomb known as KV60. In the course of those years, the tools of archaeology had become very high-tech. Scientists could now scan images of 3,500-year-old bodies, gathering far more information than had been possible in the past. In 2006, Egyptian archaeologists decided it was time to have another look at those female mummies, suspecting one of them could be the missing Hatshepsut.

Archaeologists took the two mummies to a laboratory in the basement of the Cairo Museum. After some study, experts wondered if the larger of the two women might be royalty. Her arms lay folded across her chest in the burial position used for Egyptian royalty.

Upon scanning the larger mummy, scientists found that she was missing a tooth. Archaeologists said it might have been knocked out during the embalming process. They had one of Hatshepsut's canopic jars (they knew it was hers because it was engraved with her symbol), so they scanned that too. Along with her organs, scientists discovered that the jar held a human tooth. That tooth matched the gap in the larger mummy's jaw!

**Thutmose III (right) may have overthrown his stepmother and erased her name from Egyptian writings.**

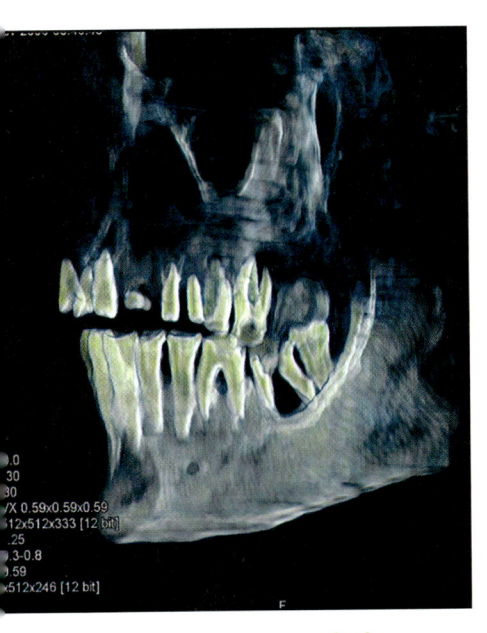

**The mummy was missing the same kind of tooth that was found in Hatshepsut's canopic jar.**

Many archaeologists were convinced that the mummy was Hatshepsut, but others argued that the tooth was not positive proof. DNA testing seemed like a good idea. Archaeologists had long ago identified the mummies of some of Hatshepsut's ancestors. By comparing DNA, they could at least know whether this mummy was a member of Hatshepsut's family.

Egyptian officials had never been fans of DNA testing on mummies. They felt it was unreliable because ancient DNA is terribly fragile and extremely difficult to collect. Worst of all, it could be easily contaminated by the DNA of the people who worked with it. However, the lab in the basement of the Cairo Museum was set up to test ancient DNA. This made the experiments simpler to do and far easier to control.

**Genetic scientists**, experts in ancient DNA, arrived with long, hollow needles to take DNA samples from the mummy's hip and thigh bones. They compared those samples to some DNA taken from the mummies of Hatshepsut's ancestors. After months of careful study, Egyptian officials came back with the announcement that the test results were extremely promising. They felt sure that the lost mummy of Hatshepsut had been found.

**Egyptian authorities agreed that the mummy's DNA should be tested.**

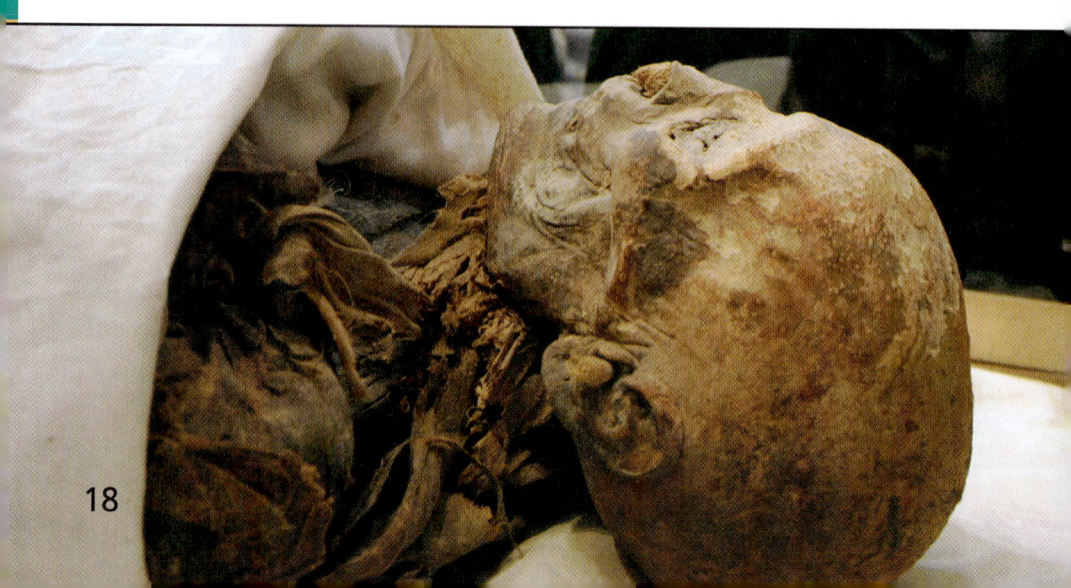

# Chapter 5  Not Every Mummy Comes from Egypt

In the ancient world, Egyptians were not the only ones mummifying their dead. Thousands of years before Hatshepsut was born, a South American culture known as the Chinchorros made mummies too.

These people were mostly fishermen who lived in what is now Chile. When a person died, the Chinchorros took the body apart, treated it with chemicals to preserve it, and then lovingly put it back together.

The Chinchorros mummies appear to be the oldest mummies yet discovered, but other cultures around the world had similar practices. In Peru, archaeologists have found mummies from the Inca culture that existed between 1100 and 1500 CE. Some suggest that the Inca mummified all their dead, not just those who were wealthy and powerful. In island caves off the Alaskan coast, centuries-old mummies of the Aleut people silently await the afterlife. Modern Aleut leaders say their people have always known of these sites and would like to see them left alone. In the American Southwest, the Anasazi sent their mummified dead off to the afterlife in new sandals. Little is known of who these people were.

**Chinchorros mummies date to around 5000 BCE.**

19

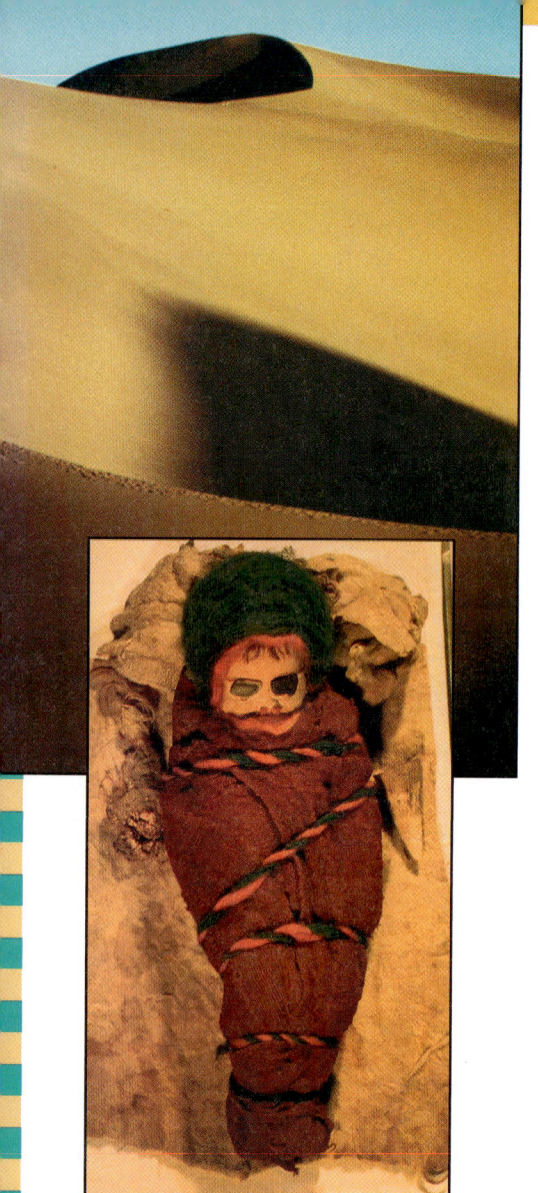

China's Taklimakan Desert has offered up some of the most remarkable mummies of all. In this extremely dry climate, archaeologists have found hundreds of almost perfectly preserved mummies. Many are about three thousand years old, around the same age as Ramesses I.

However, the first thing archaeologists noticed about these mummies was that, although they were found in Central China, they were clearly European. Reddish-brown hair falls in braids over their shoulders, and many are more than six feet tall. DNA testing links them to people who lived in England and Western Europe, but experts are not sure how they came

The Taklimakan mummies lived long before Marco Polo, the Italian explorer who told stories of the wonders of Chinese culture back to an amazed Europe in 1295 CE.

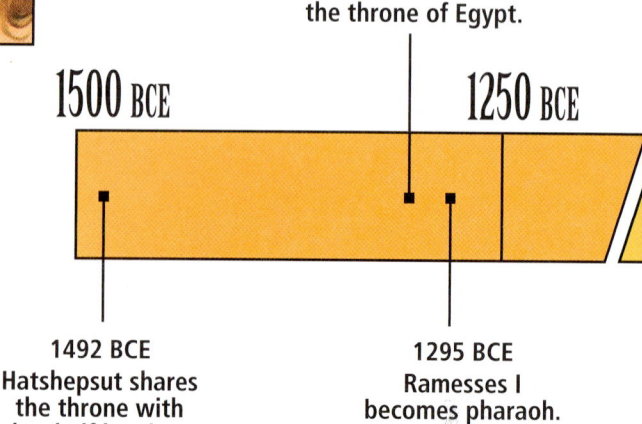

1500 BCE

1492 BCE
Hatshepsut shares the throne with her half brother.

1333 BCE
Tutankhamen takes the throne of Egypt.

1250 BCE

1295 BCE
Ramesses I becomes pharaoh.

20

to rest in the Chinese desert. Clearly, people of European descent lived there thousands of years ago. However, this discovery conflicts with long-held ideas about the time lines of Asian and European interactions. As archaeologists learn, history must be rewritten.

The Taklimakan mummies are "accidental" mummies. Remember that a mummy is a dead body that has not been allowed to decay. Decay only happens in the presence of certain elements such as water and oxygen. Extremely dry climates such as the arid climate of the Taklimakan Desert hinder decay. So does extreme cold.

In 1991 a group of hikers were making their way over a glacier high in the Oetztal Alps on the Austrian-Italian border when they saw something odd stuck in the ice. Upon closer inspection they found the long-frozen remains of a man. He wore a cape made of grass, with a bow and arrows at his side. "Oetzi," as he soon became known, had died on these remote heights and lain frozen for more than 5,000 years. His clothes and weapons, his injuries, even the contents of his stomach and his DNA offer clues to archaeologists and other scientists about a long-ago culture. One might say that he has defied death and time to tell his story.

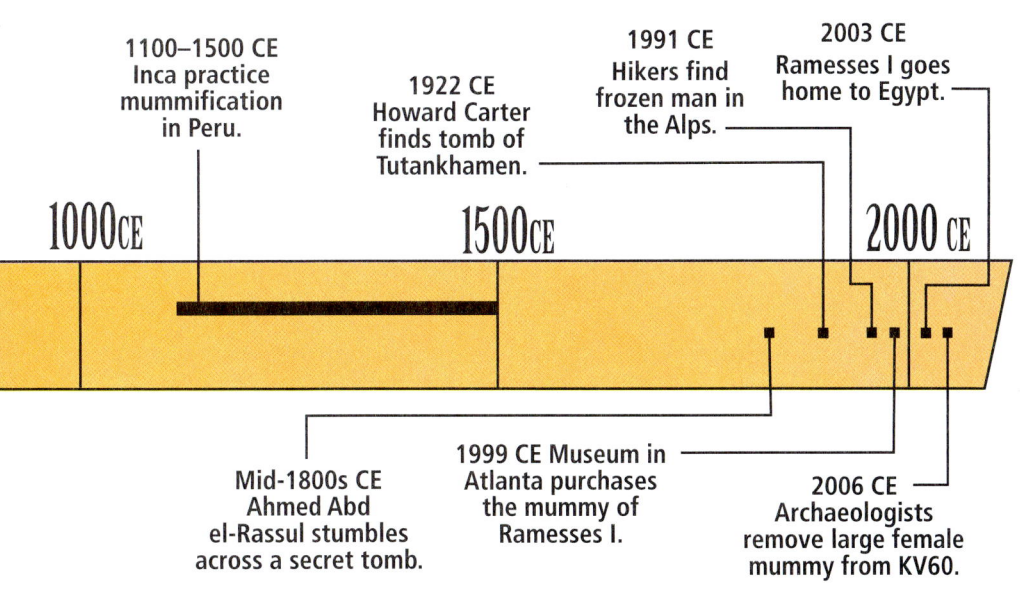

**1100–1500 CE** Inca practice mummification in Peru.

**1922 CE** Howard Carter finds tomb of Tutankhamen.

**1991 CE** Hikers find frozen man in the Alps.

**2003 CE** Ramesses I goes home to Egypt.

1000 CE        1500 CE        2000 CE

**Mid-1800s CE** Ahmed Abd el-Rassul stumbles across a secret tomb.

**1999 CE** Museum in Atlanta purchases the mummy of Ramesses I.

**2006 CE** Archaeologists remove large female mummy from KV60.

# Now Try This

Imagine that you are an archaeologist working in one of the world's great deserts, when your team uncovers a female mummy. The dry climate has left her almost perfectly preserved, but there is no written evidence of her identity. It is your job to discover who she was in life.

## Here's How To Do It!

1. Begin a notebook to help you process information about the mummy. The first entry in your notebook should be a map or drawing of the site where the mummy was found. As you sketch your map, include the name of the country, as well as geographical features such as nearby waterways or mountains.

2. Describe the moment of discovery, including events that led you to investigate this site. Note other archaeological discoveries that have happened in the area, as these may offer clues to your mummy's identity.

3. Note details about the mummy's appearance. What does she look like? Are her clothes primitive, perhaps made of grass or animal hides? Or is she dressed in robes made of woven cloth?

4. Describe artifacts found in the same area as the mummy. Was she surrounded by pottery, tools, or weapons? Did you find her in a building, a burial site, or out in the open? Were there other mummies nearby?

5. Use all the information that you and your team collected to theorize about the mummy's identity. Identify technology that you will use to prove your theory true or false.

6. Share your theory with the class. Listen and make note of your classmates' ideas about the mummy's identity.

# Glossary

**artery** *n.* waterway or road that routinely carries heavy traffic.

**artifacts** *n.* objects left over from past events.

**cross-sectioned** *adj.* seen as a slice through a solid object, showing the object's internal structure.

**embalmed** *v.* treated with chemicals to prevent tissue from decaying.

**excavated** *v.* dug out of the ground.

**genetic scientists** *n.* people who study DNA.

**influential** *adj.* able to guide or control the behavior of others.

**inscribed** *v.* carved or written.

**intrusive** *adj.* causing damage by forced entrance or action.

**pharaoh** *n.* Egyptian ruler in the ancient past.